IF FOUND PLE/

C000051314

Greater Than a Tourist Book Series
Reviews from Readers

I think the series is wonderful and beneficial for tourists to get information before visiting the city.

-Seckin Zumbul, Izmir Turkey

I am a world traveler who has read many trip guides but this one really made a difference for me. I would call it a heartfelt creation of a local guide expert instead of just a guide.

-Susy, Isla Holbox, Mexico

New to the area like me, this is a must have!

-Joe, Bloomington, USA

This is a good series that gets down to it when looking for things to do at your destination without having to read a novel for just a few ideas.

-Rachel, Monterey, USA

i

Good information to have to plan my trip to this destination.

-Pennie Farrell, Mexico

Great ideas for a port day.

-Mary Martin USA

Aptly titled, you won't just be a tourist after reading this book. You'll be greater than a tourist!

-Alan Warner, Grand Rapids, USA

Even though I only have three days to spend in San Miguel in an upcoming visit, I will use the author's suggestions to guide some of my time there. An easy read - with chapters named to guide me in directions I want to go.

-Robert Catapano, USA

Great insights from a local perspective! Useful information and a very good value!

-Sarah, USA

This series provides an in-depth experience through the eyes of a local. Reading these series will help you to travel the city in with confidence and it'll make your journey a unique one.

-Andrew Teoh, Ipoh, Malaysia

GREATER THAN A TOURIST- ATHENS GREECE

50 Travel Tips from a Local

Eleni Panagiotopoulou

Cover designed by: Ivana Stamenkovic
Cover Image: https://pixabay.com/en/temple-athens-greece-architecture-594633/

CZYK Publishing Since 2011.

Greater Than a Tourist
Visit our website at www.GreaterThanaTourist.com

Lock Haven, PA
ISBN: 9781793121813

>TOURIST

50 TRAVEL TIPS FROM A LOCAL

BOOK DESCRIPTION

Are you excited about planning your next trip?

Do you want to try something new?

Would you like some guidance from a local?

If you answered yes to any of these questions, then this Greater Than a Tourist book is for you.

Greater Than a Tourist - Athens, Greece by Eleni Panagiotopoulou gives you the inside scoop on Athens. Most travel books tell you how to travel like a tourist. Although there is nothing wrong with that, as part of the Greater Than a Tourist series, this book will give you travel tips from someone who has lived at your next travel destination.

In these pages, you will discover advice that will help you throughout your stay. This book will not tell you exact addresses or store hours but instead will give you excitement and knowledge from a local that you may not find in other smaller print travel books.

Travel like a local. Slow down, stay in one place, and get to know the people and the culture. By the time you finish this book, you will be eager and prepared to travel to your next destination.

TABLE OF CONTENTS

DEDICATION

This book is dedicated to my mother. Her name was Athina, she loved this city and she was the one to introduce me to its many delights. Thank you mum.

ABOUT THE AUTHOR

Eleni is a professional translator who has lived in Athens her whole life. Eleni loves to travel and never misses an opportunity to explore new destinations, but always stays loyal to the city that raised her and made her who she is: Athens.

HOW TO USE THIS BOOK

The Greater Than a Tourist book series was written by someone who has lived in an area for over three months. The goal of this book is to help travelers either dream or experience different locations by providing opinions from a local. The author has made suggestions based on their own experiences. Please do your own research before traveling to the area in case the suggested places are unavailable.

Travel Advisories: As a first step in planning any trip abroad, check the Travel Advisories for your intended destination.
https://travel.state.gov/content/travel/en/traveladvisories/traveladvisories.html

FROM THE PUBLISHER

Traveling can be one of the most important parts of a person's life. The anticipation and memories that you have are some of the best. As a publisher of the Greater Than a Tourist book series, as well as the popular 50 Things to Know book series, we strive to help you learn about new places, spark your imagination, and inspire you. Wherever you are and whatever you do I wish you safe, fun, and inspiring travel.

Lisa Rusczyk Ed. D.
CZYK Publishing

OUR STORY

Traveling is a passion of the "Greater than a Tourist" series creator. Lisa studied abroad in college, and for their honeymoon Lisa and her husband toured Europe. During her travels to Malta, an older man tried to give her some advice based on his own experience living on the island since he was a young boy. She was not sure if she should talk to the stranger but was interested in his advice. When traveling to some places she was wary to talk to locals because she was afraid that they weren't being genuine. Through her travels, Lisa learned how much locals had to share with tourists. Lisa created the "Greater Than a Tourist" book series to help connect people with locals. A topic that locals are very passionate about sharing.

WELCOME TO
> TOURIST

INTRODUCTION

We travel to change, not of place, but ideas.

Hippolyte Taine, 1828-1893

Athens is often cited as the cradle of Western civilization, democracy and philosophy. Despite its recent turmoil due to the financial crisis, this great city remains high on the list of places you should visit at least once in your lifetime.

The capital of Greece remains lively all through the year. For sightseeing, warm, sunny days make autumn or spring the best times to visit Athens; soaring temperatures from mid-June to late-August can be tiring. Between November and February the weather is unpredictable, ranging from crisp, bright days to rain – the compensation being a relative scarcity of tourists. In fact, it can make a lovely winter city break.

1. FIRST THINGS FIRST: HOW TO GET THERE

Let's start with the basics; Greece is an EU
country, which means that if you come from another
country, no passport is required. However, if you
come from any other place of the world, remember to
bring your passport with you. There are direct flights
to Athens from most major cities in Europe such as
London, Paris, Berlin, Rome, Madrid and
Amsterdam, many of which are operated by a major
Greek airline, Aegean Airlines.

2. CURRENCY

Apart from the EU, Greece is also a member of the
Eurozone, so the euro is the country's currency. There
are places to exchange currency in the airport, the city
centre, or you can do that in a bank. However, your
debit or credit card will also get accepted in most (if
not all) shops, hotels, restaurants etc, but your bank
may charge you an exchange fee.

3. HOW TO GET AROUND

When you arrive at the airport of Athens (named after a famous Greek politician, Eleftherios Venizelos), you have a lot of transportation options to choose from. The cheapest one, is the express buses from the airport to the city centre (X95) or to the major bus stations to other Greek cities (X93), that only cost 6 euros per person. The second cheapest option is the subway, or as we call it in Greece, the Metro. The ticket from the airport to anywhere costs 10 euros per person, but it's more reliable, faster and has more destinations than the bus. The last, and most expensive (but the most comfortable) option is the taxi. My tip is to download the Uber Taxi or the Beat Ride app and get a taxi through that, as it's impossible to get scammed this way.

4. HOTELS

Doing a quick search on the internet you will find some hotels that are in good locations, within walking distance of just about everything. You may find better hotels for less but you may not like your surroundings or find that the money you save is being spent on getting to and from the archaeological sites, shopping and dining areas. My suggestions would be Hotel Attalos, Cecil Hotel, Athens Cypria Hotel and Hotel Central for the ideal combination of economy and luxury.

5. OTHER ACCOMMODATION OPTIONS

With Airbnb on the rise, and hostels opening throughout the city, the hotel is not your only option anymore. When in Athens the desirable areas to stay in are the Plaka, Makrianni, Koukaki, Thission, Syntagma and Monastiraki. These areas all border the Acropolis and the archeological park around it. Everything you need including shops, restaurants, the metro to the ferries, buses, taxis and nightlife is within walking distance and many of the streets are pedestrian only. You can find more apartments, houses and villas outside of central Athens on Booking.com's Athens page, using the search options.

6. LEARN SOME PHRASES

In general, Greeks speak English fairly well (especially the younger generations) and can hold a conversation in English easily, but it's always nice to learn some basic, useful phrases to help you get around and understand the local culture better.

Good morning = Καλημέρα (Kaleemera) and Good evening = Καλησπέρα (Kaleespera)

This is one of the easiest greetings to learn, because it's applicable to all forms of address (formal and informal) and it's actually the most common among Greeks.

You may greet a shopkeeper or a taxi driver with a "Yásas" (Γεια σας = Hello), and you will get a welcoming "Yásas" back.

Other useful phrases might be:

I love you: S'agapo
I am a vegetarian: Eemay chortofagos
Thank you: Efcharisto
Please: Parakalo
How much is it?: Poso kanee?
Do you speak English?: Meelate angleeka?

7. THE POET

What if I told you that you could find a published poet, a really famous one, whose works have been translated into English, French, German and Italian and his best known work, "The Rubaiyat" is on the curriculum of a number of American universities and is one of the most beautiful tributes to wine and life, and he makes sandals for a living? Stavros Melissinos has touched the feet of John Lennon, Paul McCartney, Sophia Loren, Jackie Kennedy, Rudolph Nureyev, Margo Fontaine, Anthony Quinn, George Pappard, Ursula Andress, and Gary Cooper among others as he fitted them for his sandals, which are based on ancient Greek designs and are as famous as his poetry. Visit him on tiny Ag. Theklas street across from Monastiraki Square or visit his statue someday.

8. PIREAUS

For me, there is no better feeling than going to the harbor and getting on a ferry boat to sail off to a Greek island. As much as I love Athens, there is a feeling of having escaped as you sail out of the port and onto the Aegean sea and you gaze over the waves at the white sea of apartment buildings and look for those famous landmarks of the Acropolis, Lykabettus and Phillopapou or the mountains of Hymettos, Pendeli and Parnitha. If you find yourself on a ferry

steaming towards the Greek Islands I'm sure you'll
agree with me.

9. THE TEMPLE OF POSEIDON AT SOUNION

On a hill overlooking the sea at the very tip of the
Attiki Peninsula on a spot that could not be more
perfect for an ancient site of worship is the Temple of
Poseidon, God of the Sea, that boasts the carved
grafitti of Lord Byron. There is a small beach below
and a sea that looks and feels like you're in an island,
as well as two small fish tavernas and many more on
the way there and back. Go in the late afternoon, have
a swim and an ouzo and some mezedes and see the
temple and watch the sunset before going back to
Athens. It is not really in Athens but you still need to
go there. It's only an hour away by taxi.

10. BEST TIMES TO VISIT

The best times to visit Athens are between
March and May and from September to November.
Weather during these months is agreeable and
sunshine is pretty much a guarantee. Not to mention,
crowds are thinner and hotel and airfare deals are

easier to come by than in summer. But if you choose to visit between December and February, don't fret. Though chilly, Athens' winters are relatively mild, thanks in part to Greece's Mediterranean location. June through August, meanwhile, bring stifling heat and hordes of tourists, so sightseeing can be a bit uncomfortable and quite a headache at this time.

11. THE ATHENS METRO

It took us a long time, but Athens finally has the most beautiful metro system in the world and we all hope it stays this way. In the meantime, even if there is nowhere you need to go with the new metro, it is worth visiting it even if it is for a few stops (you can visit the Hilton and the American Embassy). As you may have heard, work on the metro was slow because of all the antiquities they discovered. Every time they dug a new hole they would find a grave, or a wall or an urn or something and would have to put down their picks and shovels and call in the archaeologists who would do their digging with toothbrushes, which is a bit slower. Meanwhile deep below the surface, the giant metro mouse is churning fossilized dinosaurs into microscopic chips as it tunnels it's way through

the city and hopefully coming to my neighborhood
one day.

12. NIGHTLIFE IN ATHENS

Many places close in Athens when the weather
gets warm but Stoa Athanaton in the Central Market
of Athens (in the meat section) is one of the best
places to hear authentic rembetika, if it is still open.
Also the Kallipateira has some live rembetika. In the
daytime go to Kapni Karea Cafe which is between
Metropolis and Ermou Streets in this little alley a
block down from the small church of Kapni Karea in
the middle of Ermou street. There is usually good
music going on there in the afternoon that lasts until
the early evening. The Athinorama magazine has a
listing of bars and clubs but you may want to call and
make sure a club is open before you go since many of
them are seasonal.

13. PLACES TO EAT AT PLAKA

Plaka restaurants are touristy by nature which does not always mean bad food. What it does mean is a transient clientele and some restaurants have reputations for serving food that a true Greek would send back. The restaurants I have reviewed are the ones that the people from the neighborhood eat at too. It does not mean you won't get a bad meal because that can happen anywhere. But a bad meal is far less likely if you stick to the places that the locals eat at too. Some of my favorites are "Byzantino Taverna", "Platanos Taverna", "Taverna O Psaras" and "L'Audrion Wine".

14. ALTERNATIVE TOURS OF ATHENS

Walks organised by a collective of local photographers, artists, writers, musicians, designers and architects are the perfect way to see another side of Athens. They design and operate all of their tours and activities themselves. They're not resellers of tours, like most other tour companies are.

There are tours on photography, street art, social movements, architecture – and on bikes.

15. ATHENS BUS TOURS

It is highly likely that you encounter several double decker red buses while strolling in the center of Athens, especially around Syntagma Square. For a small fee per person, you may board one of the buses and you can leave it in any of the many stops it makes along the way you'd like to explore more and then catch the next one to continue your tour. Now you can book your bus tickets online to avoid the on site hassle.

16. ATHENS UNDER THE STARS

The National Observatory of Athens must be one of my favorite spots in the city, because it's located really close to the Acropolis, in Thissio area in a beautiful, historic building on top of the hill of the Nymphs. Even if the Observatory is not open, I would suggest a walk there to enjoy the view of the Acropolis and see one of the first powerful telescopes in Greece the huge, ancient telescope "Diomides". Visit their website or call to see if there are any guided tours during your trip, and if the weather allows it (but it's Greece, the weather is usually not a

problem) you 'll get the chance to observe some of
the closest objects of the night sky.

17. BRUNCHING IN ATHENS

This might be an imported and somewhat recent
addition to the Athenian scene, but Athenians have
embraced it fully and gladly. It combines all our
favourite elements: coffee, food, drinks and endless
chit-chat with friends on a lazy Sunday afternoon. My
top spots are "Harvest Coffee & Wine", "Eat at
Milton's" and "Mama Roux".

18. ESCAPE ROOMS

Another foreign and recent fun outlet, are the
hundreds escape rooms you can find in Athens. Every
single one I've ever been to is designed to
accommodate non-Greek speakers and some are truly
a work of art! If you're fan of riddle-solving,
mystery-seeking fun, you'll definitely find one that
serves your needs in Athens. Some of the best are:
Athens Clue, The MindTrap and Sir Lock's House.

19. ACROPOLIS

The Acropolis is the one historical site you can't miss. You can take a tour or wander up there yourself but during the summer, whatever you do, unless it is overcast, go early or late in the day. It can get very hot up there and gasping for breath can take way from your ability to marvel at the greatest of all archaeological sites. Getting to the Acropolis is easy and more pleasant than ever because the large avenues which border the south and west of the site.

One way to get to the Acropolis is to walk up from the Plaka and keep climbing until you come to the small road that goes around it and head west (to your right). The entrance is up from the rock of Areopagos. The easiest way is to follow Dioysiou Aeropagitou, the large pedestrian street that starts near Hadrian's Arch and goes around the south side of the Acropolis until you come to the marble paths that lead up the hill. This road becomes Apostolou Pavlou which is also car-less and continues past the cafes of Thission to the lower Ermou and Kerameikos archaeological site which is at the bottom of Monastiraki.

20. THE ACROPOLIS MUSEUM

The new Acropolis Museum was designed to offer the best conditions for the exhibition of its exhibits. A walk through its galleries is a walk through history between the masterpieces of the Archaic and Classical periods, but also in the ancient neighborhoods of Athens whose city streets and buildings you can see below when you look through the glass floors of the museum. It was hoped that by building the Acropolis Museum, the British Museum would return the Elgin Marbles, but don't hold your breath. In the meantime there are copies of those pieces to go along with the thousands of ancient stones and statues that finally have a home, worthy of them. Don't miss this museum.

General admission fee: 5 euros.

Reduced admission fee: 3 euros.

Free admission

(Ask if you are entitled to free admission. You have to be a member of parliament, student from an EU country, a child under 5 and a few other types. If you are not allowed to get in free you may be able to get in for the reduced admission if you are a student from a non EU country or a senior citizen from an EU country).

Museum Hours:

Tuesday to Sunday: 8.00 a.m. to 8.00 p.m.

Last admission: 7.30 p.m.

Galleries cleared at 7.45 p.m.

The Museum is open every Friday until 10 p.m.

Monday: Closed.

Closed: 1 January, 25 March, Easter Sunday, 1 May, 25 December and 26 December.

To get here by metro just get off at the Acropolis stop on the red line. If you are walking it is right down from Dionysiou Areopagitou where it intersects with Makrianni Street on the south side of the Acropolis.

21. SYNTAGMA SQUARE AND KOLONAKI

Plateia Syntagma, the centre of modern Athens crowned by the large, Neo-Classical Parliament building. Standing sentry outside are the evzones - soldiers marching solemnly back and forth in traditional short skirts and pompommed shoes. By Parliament, on the wide, tree-lined avenue of Vasilissis Sofias is Museum Row, where many of Athens' finest museums are concentrated. Behind

Syntagma is posh Kolonaki, home to ambassadors, models, movie stars and the fabulous designer boutiques that cater to them. This is the prime spot for shopping, people-watching and glamorous but pricey café-sitting. Rising above it all is Lykavittos Hill, topped by a famous outdoor theatre, cafés and a restaurant with a view to die for.

22. OMONOIA AND EXARCHEIA

Exarcheia and Omonia are among Athens' most well-worn districts. Though neither qualifies as beautiful, both are steeped in history, some of it quite recent. In 1973, the Polytechnic student uprising in Exarcheia was crushed by the junta but it did eventually lead to the fall of the military dictatorship. The students left behind an area full of lively cafés; this is also the best place to hear rembetika, the gritty Greek blues. Balow Exarcheia is seedy, clamorous Omonia, and just beyond is the colourful marketplace district.

23. FESTIVALS AND EVENTS

Epiphany (6 Jan)

The "Blessing of the Waters". when ports, boats and beaches are blessed, and young men dive for crosses cast into the water by priests; it's a year's good luck for the successful divers.

Apokries (Feb-Mar)

The Greek Orthodox Carnival begins 58 days before Easter, Festivities, especially glamorous masquerade parties,

last for days. In Athens, the colourful celebrations centre on Plaka, where the streets are packed with celebrants and

masked musicians.

Clean Monday

Greeks celebrate the first day of Lent by going to the country side and flying kites. In Athens, the sky above Filopappos Hill is usually filled with them that day.

Independence Day (25 Mar)

Full-on military parades with tanks, guns and batallions celebrate the date in 1821, when after nearly 400 years of occupation, the Greek revolution successfully rose up against the Ottoman Empire.

Easter

This is the most important event on the Greek Orthdox Calenda, far outweighing Christmas. On the night of Ester Friday (Good Friday or as Greeks call it "Big Friday"), participants follow effigies of Jesus on flower-covered biers in candle-lit processions concluding in midnight service and fireworks (and, in mountain villages, rounds of gunshots). On Easter Sunday, families gather to enjoy a meal of roast lamb, and also eat eggs dyed red symbolising both the blood and the rebirth of Christ.

Athens and Epidauros Festivat (Jun-Sep)

Ancient Greeks performed their timeless tragedies in the spectacular Odeon

of Herodes Atticus and the theatre of Epidauros. Now, every summer, the world's greatest singers, dancers and actors perform under moonlight in these venues. Recent singers include the Harlem Gospel Choir, while Gérard Depardieu and Isabella Rossellini have performed in classical works at Epidauros.

Ohi Day (October 28th)

A national holiday, Ohi Day (literally "Day of No"), celebrates Greece's decisive "no" to Mussolini during World War II. A big military parade, culminating at Syntagma square, is staged in Athens.

24. ZAPPEION

The 19th-century Zappeion stands in pleasant grounds at the southern end of the National Gardens. Its tree lined paths are open to the public, while the Zappeion itself hosts international conferences.

25. PLATEIA DEXAMENI

On the top of Kolonaki, at the base of Lycabettus, stands Dexamenis Square. Greener and lower-key than Plateia Kolonaki, and home to one of Athens nicest outdoor cinemas. It was named after the famous water city of the Roman emperor Hadrian. The square is a small opening in the urban fabric surrounded by green and the verdant hill, a retreat in the city center. It has been connected with modern Greek culture and literature. At its coffee shops, many great Greek authors and poets like Souris, Papadiamantis, Varnalis, Kazantzakis and Elytis were frequent patrons.

26. NATIONAL HISTORICAL MUSEUM

Greece's first parliament building, this is now a museum specializing in the War of Independence. The National Historical Museum is permanently housed in the Old Parliament Building at Stadiou Street (Kolokotronis square) since 1960. The Museum narrates the history of Modern Greece: the period of Ottoman and Latin rule, the Greek War of Independence (1821), the liberation struggles, the creation of an independent state, the political, social and spiritual development of the Greeks up to the present day.

27. FRIDAY MORNING STREET MARKET (XENOKRATOUS STREET)

This is one of Athens' most lively fruit and vegetable markets. Most Athens neighbourhoods have a weekly laïki agora, a street market for fruit, veg and household miscellanious stuff, and Kolonaki's is a good one. Leafy Xenokratous is blocked off to traffic from Friday morning to early afternoon. Local regulars come to buy fresh fruit, vegetables, fish, olives, honey, handmade products and flowers.

28. NUMISMATIC MUSEUM

This is one of the most important museums of Greece and houses one of the greatest collections of coins, ancient and modern, in the world. The museum itself is housed in the mansion of the archaeologist Heinrich Schliemann, formally known as Iliou Melathron (Greek: Ιλίου Μέλαθρον, "Palace of Ilion").

29. MUSEUM OF THE HISTORY OF GREEK COSTUME

The Museum is exclusively devoted to Greek dress. It contains approximately 25,000 pieces, chiefly authentic regional costumes and jewellery worn throughout the Greek world. The purpose of its existence is the collection, preservation, study, and finally the highlighting of the history of the Greek costume. One of its main activities is the organization, on an annual basis, of thematic exhibitions, which afford the public the opportunity to become acquainted with a different part, each time, of the Museum's rich collection.

Since 1997 the Museum is a full member of the International Council of Museums (ICOM).

30. TOMB OF THE UNKNOWN SOLDIER

The Tomb of the Unknown Soldier contains the remains of a dead soldier who is unidentified. These remains are considered impossible to be identified, and so serve as a symbol for all of a country's unknown dead wherever they fell in the war being remembered. The anonymity of the entombed soldier is the key symbolism of the monument; it could be the tomb of anyone who fell in service of the nation, and therefore serves as a monument symbolizing all of the sacrifices.Two quotations by Thucydides, from Pericles' Funeral Oration,are inscribed on the retaining wall: Μία κλίνη κενὴ φέρεται ἐστρωμένη τῶν ἀφανῶν ("... and one bed is carried empty, made for the unknown ones"), and Ἀνδρῶν ἐπιφανῶν πᾶσα γῆ τάφος ("The whole earth is the burial ground of famous men"). The inscriptions flank a central sculpture in low relief, depicting a dying hoplite. The names of battlefields where Greeks have fought since independence are inscribed on the monument.

The monument is guarded round the clock by the Evzones of the Presidential Guard.

31. GREEK COFFEE

As "Greek Coffee" we refer to what is known to the rest of the world as "Turkish Coffee". It used to be called "Turkish Coffee" in Greece too, until the persecution of the Greeks from Constantinople in the early 1960s, when people starting referring to it as "Greek".

Thick, sweet, pungent mud of strong, black coffee. Ask for an elliniko metrio. But you will see a lot of locals drinking ice coffee, even in the winter. This could be Frappé Nescafé, milk and cold water whipped into a pleasant, cool froth, or Freddo Espresso. Freddo Espresso is kind of a Greek spin on the classic Italian coffee, but adjusted to the Greece's heat.

32. GREEK DRINKS

Ouzo: Greece wouldn't be the same without this spirit. Drunk with mezes, this aniseed-flavoured distillate packs a powerful punch.

Tsipouro: Made from the residue left after distilling Muscatel grapes, fiery, warming tsipouro does its job best in winter months.

Retsina: The taste is not subtle, but the affection for this wine with pine resin cuts across
all age and class barriers.

Krasi Hima: Home-made barrel wine, often poured into pitchers or plastic bottles directly from casks on the taverna wall.

Mavrodaphne: The name translates as "black laurel". The best grapes for this rich, dark, port-like sweet wine come from the Peloponnese.

Aghiorghitiko: Deep, velvety "St George" wines from Nemea are the rising stars of the growing Greek wine industry.

Assyrtiko Greece's finest white wine -- one of the most unusual in the Mediterranean - is redolent of honeysuckle and figs.

Savatiano Greece's most common white wine is great with seafood and salads. It is most often found in tavernas.

33. GREEK DISHES

Moussaka: There are many variations on this famous country casserole, but the basic ingredients (eggplant and minced lamb layered with potatoes and tomatoes, enriched with wine, spiced with cinnamon and topped with bechamel) stay the same. The flavour is charming and earthy.

Stifado: This rich, tender, wild rabbit stew, comes from the mountains of northern Greece, where it stills warms villagers every winter. The rabbit is spiced with cumin, cloves and cinnamon, but its most wonderful characteristic is an unusual sweetness, achieved by the addition of lots of small onions, cooked until caramelized.

Horiatiki: A bastardized version appears on menus worldwide as "Greek Salad". The real thing is just a matter of fresh ingredients. Sun-ripened tomatoes, crisp cucumbers, crunchy red onions and green peppers, rich Kalamata olives topped with a slab of feta, aromatic oregano and extra virgin olive oil make up this simple but delicious salad.

Grilled Octopus: Best caught and served on the same day, having been grilled over hot coals, topped with a sqeeze of lemon and drizzled with oil and vinegar.

The texture should be tender and the taste salty-sweet.

Pittes: Pittes came to Greece from Turkey and the Middle East. The key to perfect pittes (which means "pies") is the famous filo crust: dozens of layers of paper-thin, translucent dough, brushed with butter or olive oil, and baked to light, flaky perfection. Fillings range from sweet to savoury. Try not to miss the famous hortopita filled with spinach and wild greens.

Kokoretsi: New EU food laws have made this dish technically illegal, but in old-time tavernas, Greeks continue to serve it year-round. We take the intestines of lamb. marinate them in herbs, garlic and lemon juice, and roast the whole thing for hours over coals, until it drips with wonderful juice.

Souvlaki: Souvla means spit-roasted, and this is the Greeks' favourite way to serve meat. Souvlaki refers to the ubiquitus street favourite: hunks of chicken, pork and lamb spit-roasted for hours. They are often lathered with tzatziki, and stuffed along with onions and tomatoes into a hot, freshly baked, oiled and fried bread-dough.

34. THE BEACHES

In the south of Athens, you will find many beautiful beaches ideal for swimming, sunbathing and walking. Some of the best are:

Astir Vouliagmeni: The ultimate luxury beach experience, Astir Vouliagmeni is considered one of the top spots for a summer swim in Athens. Located – as it's name would suggest – in the chic southern suburb of Vouliagmeni, Astir offers a full range of high-quality services, from free WiFi across the beach, to the ability to pre-book one of the large and comfortable sun-loungers. And of course, a wide selection of coffees, ice creams, food and drink are all available.

All of this of course comes at a price – Astir is one of the relatively few beaches with an entrance fee which is 18 euros during the week and 28 euros on the weekends per adult. But if what you are after is some pampering (as well as some fascinating people watching) then it's worth the fee. Even despite the high price weekends can still get very busy so head there early to guarantee getting an umbrella (or prebook). The beach is open from 08:00-21:00, although you can visit the restaurant until midnight.

Kavouri: Also located in the suburb of Vouliagmeni, Kavouri is actually a pine-tree covered peninsula studded with expensive villas. There are several sandy stretches where one can swim although the most popular is Megalo Kavouri towards the tip of the western coast which is organized with sunbeds for rent as well as free areas. As on many beaches, here you will also find many people playing 'raketes' or beach paddle ball (a national sport in Greece) in the open space behind the beach.

The beach is sandy and the water shallow for quite a distance and there are a number of places to buy refreshments. The beach is also relatively easy to get to via public transport: take the metro to Elliniko station and from there the 122 bus.

Vouliagmeni Lake: Not quite a beach but a rare geological formation located next to the sea. The waters of the lake are fed up by saltwater via underground currents, through the mountain (although there is still some mystery about how this occurs). Near the sun-beds the water is quite shallow although at the opposite end they sink to unknown depths. In the lake the waters are often slightly warmer than in the sea, so it is particularly popular earlier in the season. Generally peaceful and quiet, it is a good option if you want easy access to plenty of amenities without the thump of a nearby beach-bar.

The facilities of the lake include the all-day bar, restaurant, changing rooms, showers and full wheelchair access. It is also worth staying for a drink in the evening when the rock walls are lit up and soft music floats out over the still waters.

Voula: One of the most popular spots to swim in Athens itself located in the southern suburb of Voula. The sandy beach offers a range of services and has high-quality sunbeds at reasonable prices. During the summer, beach parties are also often organized with performances by well-known Greek singers.

Entrance during weekdays is 4 euros per head and 5 euros over the weekend. The beach is also easily accessible via public transport: either take the metro to Elliniko station and then the 122 bus or take the tram to the terminal stop of Asklipio Voulas.

Yabanaki Varkiza: Not just a beach but a beach park with a full suite of services and amusements, located in the southern suburb of Varkiza. Here you will find a range of options for coffee, refreshments, fast food or seafood meze and ouzo. A full range of water sports is also available from waterskiing and banana boats to stand-up paddleboarding and windsurfing lessons. In the afternoons a fully supervised play area with numerous large bouncy castles also operates for children.

During the weekdays the entrance fee is 5 euros per head including an umbrella and sun loungers. On the weekends the entrance fee is 6 euros and you have to pay an additional 5 for an umbrella (although if you want just a late swim however entrance after 7pm is free). To get there via public transport take the metro to the Elliniko station and then the 171 bus or the 122 bus.

Edem: The closest beach to the city center of Athens is Edem, a long sandy beach located near the boundary between the districts of Palio Faliro and

Alimos. It is organized although as would be expected by its central location it also frequently gets busy. Aside from swimmers the area is also popular with people walking along the long seafront promenade that will take you to another two smaller beaches. Along the way you will also find a large chessboard built into the pavement where locals battle it out as they enjoy the warm weather and sea-breeze. From downtown the beach is easy to reach via tram (Edem stop).

Beach of Sounio: An organized beach with umbrellas and all kinds of amenities, what really sets this swimming spot apart is its fantastic view of the Temple of Poseidon that makes you feel like you are soaking up ancient Greek culture even as you sun yourself on a comfortable sun lounger. Some parts are organized while others are still free for the public. The crystal clear waters make it up for the 1 hour long drive. Keep in mind that in August, there is little parking space. The tavernas near the beach make great seafood meze dishes.

35. THISSION

Thission is named after the ancient temple in the Agora that is actually a temple to Hephaestus but was mistakenly called the Temple to Theseus, the mythical founder-king of Athens. By the time they had realized their mistake the neighborhood around the temple had already been called Thission. So rather than change the name of the neighborhood or lie and tell people that it was a Temple of Theseus, they decided to not say anything and hope nobody would notice. The neighborhood of Thission, which used to be full of the furnaces of the metal workers, would have been more aptly named Hephaestion, for Hephaestus who was the God of fire and the patron of all craftsmen. Instead it has existed for centuries named after Theseus, the founder of Athens, who had gone to Crete to kill the minotaur.

Thission used to be a place where few people went, especially tourists. Except for the temple you would barely see it mentioned in the guidebooks. But it is a fun neighborhood and the pedestrianization of Apostolou Pavlou and Dionysiou Areopagitou, the roads that border the area of the Acropolis, more cafes have opened and it is almost an extension of Monastiraki, beginning where Adrianou Street ends

45

by the Thission Metro Station. If you walk up
Apostolou Pavlou with the Acropolis on your left,
past the tables of hippy craftspeople, the
neighborhood of Thission is on your right beyond the
cafes with their view of the Acropolis that tourists
have now discovered to be a sort of less congested
lower Adrianou Street. But it is actually a mix of
tourists, young Greeks and others in the cafes which
are open year around. In the summer there is a small
outdoor movie theater called Cinema Thission, at
Apostolou Pavlou 7 which is open from May to
September and has the added attraction of a view of
the Acropolis.

36. PLAKA

The Plaka is the oldest section of Athens. Most of
the streets have been closed to automobile traffic,
though you should still keep a watchful eye for a
speeding motorcycle or delivery truck. At one time it
was the nightclub district, but most of these closed
down when the government outlawed amplified
music in the neighborhood in the seventies in an
effort to get rid of undesirables. The strategy was very
successful and it is now an area of restaurants,

Jewelry stores tourist shops, and cafes. Though it is quite commercialized it is still a neighborhood and arguably the nicest neighborhood in central Athens. Most of the restaurants are typical tourist places but the quality of food is not bad in some of them and if you follow my leads in the restaurant section of this guide you should have a few enjoyable evenings and not be unpleasantly surprised by the bill or wake up with a gastro-intestinal disorder on the day you were supposed to visit the Acropolis.

37. PLACES TO SHOP

If you start at the top of Syntagma Square and walk down the steps and past the fountain, at the bottom of the square is the beginning of Ermou Street, a paradise for those who live to shop. From the Parliament building you can make a straight line that follows Ermou all the way to The Gazi, the old gas works of Athens, now the center of its nightlife. Ermou street is a commercial avenue which has been turned into a pedestrian only street (besides the occasional motorcycle or taxi coming from the Hotel Electra or Athens Cypria). It is the primary clothing shopping street for Athens and contains many of the

47

big international names like Benneton, Marks & Spencer, H&M, Zara, Berksha, Sepura, and a bunch of other stores that you have probably heard of but mean nothing to me. The Greek department store, Fokas, is near the top of Ermou in a beautiful old neo-classic building that looks like it would be more suitable housing a museum and is worth a visit, even if you are not buying anything, so you can see what a Greek department store is like. The Hondos Center is also of interest, especially for women, since you may not have experienced anything like it before. It is a giant cosmetic store with other items of interest to women, sort of a department store crossed with a Walgreens. It even has a cafe.

Three quarters of the way down Ermou, right in the middle of the street, actually lower than the street, sits the small church of Kapnikarea. Here you will find those people who have tired of shopping, usually husbands or bored boyfriends, catching their breath as they sit on the stone wall that surrounds the historic church, waiting for wives and girlfriends whose stamina exceeds their own. Were they to go half a block further on the left, there is a small alley with a cafe, also called Kapnikarea, where they could drink ouzo, raki, beer, wine or soft drinks, and eat while listening to authentic live rembetika and laika music through the afternoon and into the early evening, perhaps not caring if their mates ever return from shopping. As you continue down Ermou past beautiful neo-classic buildings that have been newly restored after being set on fire by rampaging youngsters in December of 2008, you will come to Aeolou Street, another pedestrian shopping street that connects the Plaka with the Central Market(Agora) and eventually becomes Patission Street a block from Omonia Square. You can turn right on Aeolou and walk 15 minutes and be at the National Archaeology Museum, passing Ethnikis Andistassis Square, (also known as Dimarchos Square because this is where City Hall is).

38. BE A GREEK (EVEN IF IT'S FOR A DAY)

One of my favourite things to do in Athens is joining group-tours of the city and enjoying its many hidden delights like a tourist. "Be A Greek" is a local, Athenian company that specializes in Experiential Travel, a form of tourism in which Travelers focus on experiencing a country, city or particular place by connecting to its history, people and culture. They concentrate our efforts in producing quality travel, responding to the particular needs of present times while anticipating the demands of the future, having as our ultimate goal to exceed your expectations. As a local that has gone to almost all their tours, I highly recommend that you find one during your stay and book it on their website.

39. APPS TO DOWNLOAD

Beat:

If you ask a Greek whether they use Uber, you may get some funny looks. UberX does exist in Greece, but Athens is still a hardcore taxi city, and Taxibeat combines the best of both. The app finds your location using GPS, and allows you to call any of the nearby drivers based not only on their location but also on their rating from other passengers, and other criteria such as whether they speak other languages or if their car is smoke-free (unfortunately not always a given). You can set up your account to pay via Credit/Debit Card, and then review the driver when you're finished. Similar to Uber, expect you can also hail a Beat cab - they have stickers on the side of the car - and that way you know you're in safe hands.

OASA telematics:

The Greek public transport industry is trying to keep up with the technology, and luckily it has become a lot more user friendly - so if you're up for tackling the extensive Athens bus system, never fear. This app pinpoints your location and will show you nearby bus stops, along with which buses stop there, their schedule and their route. Unfortunately its live updates in real time seem to struggle a little bit with the traffic variations, but the app shows you where the bus is that moment and an estimated arrival time.

AthensBook:

This is the best app for the most basic needs you might have during a trip to Athens - it will help you find anything from the nearest supermarket, the closest bars and pastry shops, reports on local traffic and what films are playing at local cinemas. AthensBook also includes information on the closest open pharmacy (which can be very useful at night!), though in an emergency doctoranytime can find you a real doctor, though unfortunately only in Greek. AthensBook also includes information on transport - the nearest metro/tram stops, and any possible strikes. It needs the internet to find what it closest to you at the moment, but if you have a wifi or data connection it will find the answer to nearly any query.

e-table.gr:

When you've found the best place to eat in Athens, avoid disappointment by making sure to book in advance. If your Greek isn't quite up to reserving a table over the phone, e-table.gr lets you make the booking straight from your phone. This is the Greek version of OpenTable that includes photos and reviews in addition to instant and free reservations. On the other hand, for the AirBnB-ers who are struck by a late-night snack attack, e-food.gr is your best friend. The app displays reviews from other users, and also shows you estimated time for delivery, so you can make your choice based on how desperate you are for something fast.

40. SWEET CRAVINGS

Greek desserts, oriental influenced, are famous worldwide for the rich flavor, the nutritious values and the variety of alterations. There are numerous categories and types of delectable Greek Sweets, but I will list the ones that are truly authentic and popular.

Baklava: Greek Baklava is a rich, sweet pastry made of layers of filo filled with chopped nuts) and sweetened and held together with syrup or honey.

Loukoumades (Honey Puffs): Loukoumades are a popular Greek sweets. They are golden balls of fried dough that are bathed in sweet syrup and sprinkled with cinnamon and walnuts.

Kataifi: Kataifi, along with Baklava is one of the most popular and delicious Greek Desserts. It is made with a special type of pastry called kataifi or kadaifi.

Galaktompoureko (Milk Pie): Considering that this recipe include phyllo dough, takes more time for preparing, but at the end you'll see that worth it. This is nothing else but layers of crispy, buttery, flaky pastry.

41. GREEK NAMES

In modern Greece, personal names generally consist of a given name, a patronymic and a family name. Since antiquity, there has been a strong tradition of naming the first son after the paternal grandfather and the second after the maternal grandfather. This results in a continuation of names in the family line.

There is a strong clustering of first names by locality according to patron saints, famous churches or monasteries. Examples include:

Spyridon and Spyridoula in Corfu,

Gerasimos in Kefalonia,

Dionysia and Dionysios in Zakynthos,

Andreas and Andriana in Patras,

Markella and Markos in the Aegean Islands, long under Venetian rule,

Savvas among families from Asia Minor,

Emmanuel or Manolis, Joseph or Sifis, Manousos, and Mēnas in Crete.

Tsambikos or Tsampika/Mika in Rhodes.

When Greek names are used in other languages, they are sometimes rendered phonetically, such as my name for example: Eleni for Ἑλένη, and sometimes by their equivalents, like Helen in English or Hélène in French.

42. BOTANICAL GARDEN

In the Diomidis Botanical Garden, an ecosystem has been created in which wild and forest cultivated species grow and flourish. This makes it one of the world's rarest Botanical Gardens. Cultivated sections are divided into thematic and geographic units. Particularly interesting is the section of Historic plants, with species mentioned by Greek mythology as well as the Old Testament! For example, Laurus Nobilis is cultivated, dedicated to the god Apollo, the Hedera Helix, dedicated to the god Dionysus, the Ferula Communis, in whose stem Prometheus hid the fire to he conceals secretly from the gods to the people.

43. BRUNCH IN ATHENS

Whether your plan is to wander around Athens' ancient monuments or along the shady narrow streets of Greece's capital city, start the day with a good breakfast. Here are the best places to stop for a morning meal or a light bite.

Mama Roux: A popular and trendy haunt in the heart of Athens, Mama Roux has tables on the pedestrian street of Aiolou, near Agia Irene Square. Sunday brunch includes Eggs Benedict, muffins, bagels, omelets, pancakes, scrambled eggs, and burgers, all served quickly by friendly staff. The portions are large, but there is an option to have half portion dishes if you ask.

Harvest Coffee Shop and Wine: A wine bar-restaurant based on the Spanish culinary tradition, this is a small rustic joint with a friendly atmosphere. Harvest's brunch is served every day from 9 am until 7:30 pm and is a great way to start the day with a wide range of eggs (try the huevo de corral eggs) and pancakes filled with sweet and savory treats.

Acropolis Museum Restaurant: Located on the rooftop of the Acropolis Museum this restaurant offers a breathtaking view of the archaeological site as well as a great brunch menu. Thessaloniki bagels with graviera cheese, fresh milk with oats and currants, pancakes with syrup and tahini, fried eggs with syglino sausage from Mani and milk pie are just some of the Greek breakfast options.

44. THE CRISIS

Despite criticism that Athens' 2004 Olympics were a crystallisation of Greek economic dysfunction, partly responsible for today's debt crisis, Olympics spending definitely modernised the city. The new metro with the latest rolling stock, ticketing systems and automated station access dramatically improved the city's gridlocked transport system – a 90-minute cross-city trip now takes six minutes.

Despite the hardships it has weathered recently — from economic calamity to the refugee crisis — this ancient city is an astonishingly fun place to be right now, thanks to the young artists, dreamers, and entrepreneurs who have taken matters into the their own hands and started building the Athens they want to live in.

Of all the examples of crisis-era entrepreneurship, one of the most heartwarming is the rise of cooperative cafés. The traditional Athenian coffee shop, or kafeneío, has been a fixture here since the Ottoman occupation. For many people, it's a second home — a place to hash out family problems, play backgammon, enjoy the day's first drink. It is of course also where you take your coffee, which in the summer is Nescafé whirred with sugar and ice into the classic Greek frappé.

In Athens, mom-and-pop kafeneía, with their straw-seat chairs and cheap table wine in metal carafes, have been overtaken by bigger, slicker establishments. But the economic crisis has given this traditional staple of Greek culture a new lease on life. A few years ago, unemployed and overeducated young Greeks began opening their own austerity-era versions of Greek coffee shops. Helped in part by a new business law, they pooled whatever money they had or could borrow, raided their home kitchens, used humble local ingredients, and split whatever they made.

45. ANAFIOTIKA: THE HIDDEN ISLAND IN ATHENS

Anafiotika is a hidden wonder inside the bustling metropolis that is Athens. It's hard to believe a place like this even exists–a slice of the Greek Islands that is a veritable oasis amidst city noise, concrete and graffiti.

Yet somehow, despite a financial crisis, increasing urbanization and lack of government funding, Anafiotika is still going strong, retaining its distinct identify and thriving as the best little-known spot in Greece's capital.

Anafiotika is located at the base of the North end of the acropolis, but it can be tricky to find. You're technically heading for Stratonos Street but if you need a place to plug into your GPS try the Agios Georgios church at Stratonos, Athina 105 55-58, Greece.If you're hungry want to have lunch on the way, look for "Anafiotika Cafe" or "Yiasemi." These two restaurants are adjacent to each other at the base of stairs leading straight up into Anafiotika. The workers are asked for directions more times than they're asked "where's the restroom?" so they're very familiar and able to direct you further.

From the base of the stairs, you go up about a block, turn left and then walk down an alleyway leading you to Anafiotika. It all feels very strange, and you might get nervous that you've made a wrong turn. If so, you're in the right place.

46. SPORTS IN GREECE

Football in particular has seen a rapid transformation, with the Greek national football team winning the 2004 UEFA European Football Championship. Many Greek athletes have also achieved significant success and have won world and olympic titles in numerous sports during the years, such as basketball, wrestling, water polo, athletics, weightlifting, with many of them becoming international stars inside their sports. The successful organisation of the Athens 2004 Olympic Games led also to the further development of many sports and has led to the creation of many world class sport venues all over Greece and especially in Athens.

So if you're a fan of football, you can count on your nearest coffee shop or bar to stream the Sunday's Champions League match or any other major event. But if you're into baseball or cricket, you are going to have a harder time finding a place to enjoy a game of your favourite sport unfortunately.

47. CASINO IN ATHENS (PARNITHA)

Regency Casino Mont Parnes in Athens offers a beautiful setting in the heart of the Parnitha National Forest. Just 17 kilometres from the centre of Athens, it promises entertainment in a luxurious and hospitable environment.

Hours:
Monday - Friday:
Table games: 12:00 - 06:00
Slots & Touch bet: 24hrs
Saturday - Sunday:
24 hours a day
Poker Room:
Daily: 15:00 - 06:00

Conditions for admission
You must be over 21 years of age to enter. To register, you only need a European ID card or valid passport.

Entry to the casino takes place without a ticket.

Admission to the Regency Casino Mont Parnes requires proper attire and the establishment reserves the right to refuse admission to anyone not suitably dressed. Those wearing T-shirts, vests, sandals or flip-flops, sandals with socks, work clothes and track suits will not be admitted.

48. STAVROS NIARCHOS FOUNDATION CULTURAL CENTER

Designed by the architectural firm Renzo Piano Building Workshop (RPBW), the SNFCC is a sustainable, world-class cultural, educational and recreational urban complex that includes new facilities for the National Library of Greece and the Greek National Opera, located within the Stavros Niarchos Park.

The SNFCC is one of the world's most sustainable building complexes of its size. In November 2016, the SNFCC achieved the highest and most stringent international standard for sustainable design and construction - the Platinum LEED – for its innovative architecture and green technology. The platinum

LEED certification is awarded by the U.S. Green Building Council (USGBC).

49. EXPRESSIONS & COLLOQUIALISMS

The true variety and creativity of Greek phrases becomes apparent once you learn enough of the language to start speaking it with any level of competence and start throwing colloquial phrases around.

Some of them make no sense when translated, some are impossible to explain even by the Greeks. Most of them are hilarious, but simultaneously too filthy to be printable, so I give you a family-friendly selection below lest you feel like trying out the language on your visit.

Ta matia sou dekatessera (Your eyes fourteen):

A Greek phrase that instructs you to have your eyes fourteen. It means to pay close attention, keep your eyes peeled which if you think about it, doesn't make sense either.

Tha fas xilo! (You'll eat wood):

A common threat brandished by mothers and grannies to errant little children, telling them they'll eat wood means they'll get a smack. Used mostly as a threat, at least in the cities, where smacking children in public is rapidly going out of fashion.

Pias to avgo kai kourefto (Grab an egg and shave it):

Not even the Greeks know the origins of this phrase. Used to describe a Catch 22 situation, or something you can't make sense of.

Fagame to gaidaro, mas emeine i oura (We ate the donkey, just the tail is left):

Meaning we've done most of the hard work, now just a few details are left.

50. WHAT DOES ATHENS TEACH YOU?

In a city that's been populated for over 3000 years, you will not be left wondering why:

Really close to the sea and with mountains all around it, it's really the perfect place for a big city. Whether it's also a beautiful city or not is up to discussion. Many of the historical buildings that once stood proud in the city center gave their place to cemented multiple-floored buildings. The overwhelming majority of buildings in Athens were constructed during a boom in 1960s-1970s. What is taught in Urban Planning books in universities gives a socioeconomic explanation for the situation.

Nevertheless, the atmosphere remains amazing but I could say that Greeks are generally hospitable and positive, so Athens is no exception to the rule.

Athens is worldwide known as the city that never sleeps, and this is true. Every Friday and Saturday night, the streets are full of people, who want to have fun until dawn. It is not unusual to find a traffic jam in Athens Center even at 4 o'clock in the morning! Even during the week, you can find many bars full of people that stay open until late at night. The bars in Athens are literally numerous and perfect for the ultimate bar-hopping, but the most impressive thing is that they are not gathered in a single place. The districts of Athens, where you can find bars and clubs to drink and dance, are innumerable, in Athens Center but also in the suburbs.

In general, you can have a good time even if you are not into history and archaeology, it is still amusing to see how ruins blend with everything else in the city.

The historical center is wonderful. There are lots of sights, excellent restaurants and bars, you can enjoy some great walks between Syntagma and

65

Kolonaki square. Lots of folk items as well as amazing exclusive shopping, clothes accessories, and some of the most well designed jewelry. A great walk at the historical old town of Plaka under Acropolis.

If you are not afraid to explore further, there are some wonderful locations nearby by the sea, at Pasalimani, Mikrolimano, etc. with a couple of Michelin star fish restaurants. If you visit in the summer you can just jump on the Tram and visit some very nice but rather crowded beaches.

And if you are considering living in Athens long term, it is awesome. You will not miss anything at all.

>TOURIST

BONUS BOOK

50 THINGS TO KNOW ABOUT PACKING LIGHT FOR TRAVEL

PACK THE RIGHT WAY EVERY TIME

AUTHOR: MANIDIPA BHATTACHARYYA

Edited by Melanie Howthorne

ABOUT THE AUTHOR

Manidipa Bhattacharyya is a creative writer and editor, with an education in English literature and Linguistics. After working in the IT industry for seven long years she decided to call it quits and follow her heart instead. Manidipa has been ghost writing, editing, proof reading and doing secondary research services for many story tellers and article writers for about three years. She stays in Kolkata, India with her husband and a busy two year old. In her own time Manidipa enjoys travelling, photography and writing flash fiction.

Manidipa believes in travelling light and never carries anything that she couldn't haul herself on a trip. However, travelling with her child changed the scenario. She seemed to carry the entire world with her for the baby on the first two trips. But good sense prevailed and she is again working her way to becoming a light traveler, this time with a kid.

INTRODUCTION

He who would travel happily
must travel light.

-Antoine de Saint-Exupéry

Travel takes you to different places from seas and mountains to deserts and much more. In your travels you get to interact with different people and their cultures. You will, however, enjoy the sights and interact positively with these new people even more, if you are travelling light.

When you travel light your mind can be free from worry about your belongings. You do not have to spend precious vacation time waiting for your luggage to arrive after a long flight. There is be no chance of your bags going missing and the best part is that you need not pay a fee for checked baggage.

People who have mastered this art of packing light will root for you to take only one carry-on, wherever you go. However, many people can find it really hard to pack light. More so if you are travelling with children. Differentiating between "must have" and "just in case" items is the starting point. There will be ample shopping avenues at your destination which are just waiting to be explored.

71

This book will show you 'packing' in a new 'light' –
pun intended – and help you to embrace light
packing practices for all of your future travels.

Off to packing!

DEDICATION

I dedicate this book to all the travel buffs that I know,
who have given me great insights into the contents of
their backpacks.

THE RIGHT TRAVEL GEAR

1. CHOOSE YOUR TRAVEL GEAR CAREFULLY

While selecting your travel gear, pick items that are
light weight, durable and most importantly, easy to
carry. There are cases with wheels so you can drag
them along – these are usually on the heavy side
because of the trolley. Alternatively a backpack that
you can carry comfortably on your back, or even a
duffel bag that you can carry easily by hand or sling
across your body are also great options. Whatever
you choose, one thing to keep in mind is that the
luggage itself should not weigh a ton, this will give
you the flexibility to bring along one extra pair of
shoes if you so desire.

2. CARRY THE MINIMUM NUMBER OF BAGS

Selecting light weight luggage is not everything. You need to restrict the number of bags you carry as well. One carry-on size bag is ideal for light travel. Most carriers allow one cabin baggage plus one purse, handbag or camera bag as long as it slides under the seat in front. So technically, you can carry two items of luggage without checking them in.

3. PACK ONE EXTRA BAG

Always pack one extra empty bag along with your essential items. This could be a very light weight duffel bag or even a sturdy tote bag which takes up minimal space. In the event that you end up buying a lot of souvenirs, you already have a handy bag to stuff all that into and do not have to spend time hunting for an appropriate bag.

I'm very strict with my packing and have everything in its right place. I never change a rule. I hardly use anything in the hotel room. I wheel my own wardrobe in and that's it.

Charlie Watts

CLOTHES & ACCESSORIES

4. PLAN AHEAD

Figure out in advance what you plan to do on your trip. That will help you to pick that one dress you need for the occasion. If you are going to attend a wedding then you have to carry formal wear. If not, you can ditch the gown for something lighter that will be comfortable during long walks or on the beach.

5. WEAR THAT JACKET

Remember that wearing items will not add extra luggage for your air travel. So wear that bulky jacket that you plan to carry for your trip. This saves space and can also help keep you warm during the chilly flight.

6. MIX AND MATCH

Carry clothes that can be interchangeably used to reinvent your look. Find one top that goes well with a couple of pairs of pants or skirts. Use tops, shirts and jackets wisely along with other accessories like a scarf or a stole to create a new look.

7. CHOOSE YOUR FABRIC WISELY

Stuffing clothes in cramped bags definitely takes its toll which results in wrinkles. It is best to carry wrinkle free, synthetic clothes or merino tops. This will eliminate the need for that small iron you usually bring along.

8. DITCH CLOTHES PACK UNDERWEAR

Pack more underwear and socks. These are the things that will give you a fresh feel even if you do not get a chance to wear fresh clothes. Moreover these are easy to wash and can be dried inside the hotel room itself.

9. CHOOSE DARK OVER LIGHT

While picking your clothes choose dark coloured ones. They are easy to colour coordinate and can last longer before needing a wash. Accidental food spills and dirt from the road are less visible on darker clothes.

10. WEAR YOUR JEANS

Take only one pair of Jeans with you, which you should wear on the flight. Remember to pick a pair that can be worn for sightseeing trips and is equally eloquent for dinner. You can add variety by adding light weight cargoes and chinos.

11. CARRY SMART ACCESSORIES

The right accessory can give you a fresh look even with the same old dress. An intelligent neck-piece, a couple of bright scarves, stoles or a sarong can be used in a number of ways to add variety to your clothing. These light weight beauties can double up as a nursing cover, a light blanket, beach wear, a modesty cover for visiting places of worship, and also makes for an enthralling game of peek-a-boo.

12. LEARN TO FOLD YOUR GARMENTS

Seasoned travellers all swear by rolling their clothes for compact and wrinkle free packing. Bundle packing, where you roll the clothes around a central object as if tying it up, is also a popular method of compact and wrinkle free packing. Stacking folded clothes one on top of another is a big no-no as it makes creases extreme and they are difficult to get rid of without ironing.

13. WASH YOUR DIRTY LAUNDRY

One of the ways to avoid carrying loads of clothes is to wash the clothes you carry. At some places you might get to use the laundry services or a Laundromat but if you are in a pinch, best solution is to wash them yourself. If that is the plan then carrying quick drying clothes is highly recommended, which most often also happen to be the wrinkle free variety.

14. LEAVE THOSE TOWELS BEHIND

Regular towels take up a lot of space, are heavy and take ages to dry out. If you are staying at hotels they will provide you with towels anyway. If you are travelling to a remote place, where the availability of towels look doubtful, carry a light weight travel towel of viscose material to do the job.

15. USE A COMPRESSION BAG

Compression bags are getting lots of recommendation now days from regular travellers. These are useful for saving space in your luggage when you have to pack bulky dresses. While packing for the return trip, get help from the hotel staff to arrange a vacuum cleaner.

FOOTWEAR

16. PUT ON YOUR HIKING BOOTS

If you have plans to go hiking or trekking during your trip, you will need those bulky hiking boots. The best way to carry them is to wear them on flight to save space and luggage weight. You can remove the boots once inside and be comfortable in your socks.

17. PICKING THE RIGHT SHOES

Shoes are often the bulkiest items, along with being the dainty if you are a female. They need care and take up a lot of space in your luggage. It is advisable therefore to pick shoes very carefully. If you plan to do a lot of walking and site seeing, then wearing a pair of comfortable walking shoes are a must. For more formal occasions you can carry durable, light weight flats which will not take up much space.

18. STUFF SHOES

If you happen to pack a pair of shoes, ensure you utilize their hollow insides. Tuck small items like rolled up socks or belts to save space. They will also be easy to find.

TOILETRIES

19. STASHING TOILETRIES

Carry only absolute necessities. Airline rules dictate that for one carry-on bag, liquids and gels must be in 3.4 ounce (100ml) bottles or less, and must be packed in a one quart zip-lock bag. If you are planning to stay in a hotel, the basic things will be provided for you. It's best is to buy the rest from the local market at your destination.

20. TAKE ALONG TAMPONS

Tampons are a hard to find item in a lot of countries. Figure out how many you need and pack accordingly. For longer stays you can buy them online and have them delivered to where you are staying.

21. GET PAMPERED BEFORE YOU TRAVEL

Some avid travellers suggest getting a pedicure and manicure just the day before travelling. This not only gives you a well kept look, you also save the trouble of packing nail polish. Remember, every little bit of weight reduced adds up.

ELECTRONICS

22. LUGGING ALONG ELECTRONICS

Electronics have a large role to play in our lives today. Most of us cannot imagine our lives away from our phones, laptops or tablets. However while travelling, one must consider the amount of weight these electronics add to our luggage. Thankfully smart phones come along with all the essentials tools like a camera, email access, picture editing tools and more. They are smart to the point of eliminating the need to carry multiple gadgets. Choose a smart phone that suits all your requirements and travel with the world in your palms or pocket.

23. REDUCE THE NUMBER OF CHARGERS

If you do travel with multiple electronic devices, you will have to bear the additional burden of carrying all their chargers too. Check if a single charger can be used for multiple devices. You might also consider investing in a pocket charger. These small devices support multiple devices while keeping you charged on the go.

24. TRAVEL FRIENDLY APPS

Along with smart phones come numerous apps, which are immensely helpful in our travels. You name it and you have an app for it at hand – take pictures, sharing with friends and family, torch to light dark roads, maps, checking flight/train times, find hotels and many other things. Use these smart alternatives to traditional items like books to eliminate weight and save space.

I get ideas about what's essential when packing my suitcase.

-Diane von Furstenberg

TRAVELLING WITH KIDS

25. BRING ALONG THE STROLLER

Kids might enjoy walking for a while but they soon tire out and a stroller is the just the right thing for them to rest in while you continue your tour. Strollers also double duty as a luggage carrier and shopping bag holder. Remember to pick a light weight, easy to handle brand of stroller. Better yet, find out in advance if you can rent a stroller at your destination.

26. BRING ONLY ENOUGH DIAPERS FOR YOUR TRIP

Diapers take up a lot of space and add to the weight of your luggage. Therefore it is advisable to carry just enough diapers to last through the trip and a few for afterwards, till you buy fresh stock at your destination. Unless of course you are travelling to a really remote area, in which case you have no choice but to carry the load. Otherwise diapers are something you will find pretty easily.

27. TAKE ONLY A COUPLE OF TOYS

Children are easily attracted by new things in their environment. While travelling they will find numerous 'new' objects to scrutinize and play with. Packing just one favorite toy is enough, or if there is no favorite toy leave out all of them in favor of stories or imaginary games.

28. CARRY KID FRIENDLY SNACKS

Create a small snack counter in your bag to store away quick bites for those sudden hunger pangs. Depending on the child's age this could include chocolates, raisins, dry fruits, granola bars or biscuits. Also keep a bottle of water handy for your little one.

These things do not add much weight and can be adjusted in a handbag or knapsack.

29. GAMES TO CARRY

Create some travel specific, imaginary games if you have slightly grown up children, like spot the attractions. Keep a coloring book and colors handy for in-flight or hotel time. Apps on your smart phone can keep the children engaged with cartoons and story books. Older children are often entertained by games available on phones or tablets. This cuts the weight of luggage down while keeping the kids entertained.

30. LET THE KIDS CARRY THEIR LOAD

A good thing is to start early sharing of responsibilities. Let your child pick a bag of his or her choice and pack it themselves. Keep tabs on what they are stuffing in their bags by asking if they will be using that item on the trip. It could start out being just an entertainment bag initially but with growing years they will learn to sort the useful from the superfluous. Children as little as four can maneuver a small trolley suitcase like a pro- their experience in pull along toys credit. If you are worried that you may be pulling it for them, you may want to start with a backpack.

31. DECIDE ON LOCATION FOR CHILDREN TO SLEEP

While on a trip you might not always get a crib at your destination, and carrying one will make life all the more difficult. Instead call ahead to see if there are any cribs or roll out beds for children. You may even put blankets on the floor. Weave them a story about camping and they will gladly sleep without any trouble.

32. GET BABY PRODUCTS DELIVERED AT YOUR DESTINATION

If you are absolutely paranoid about not getting your favourite variety of diaper or brand of baby food, check out online stores like amazon.com for services in your destination city. You can buy things online ahead of your travel and get them delivered to your hotel upon arrival.

33. FEEDING NEEDS OF YOUR INFANTS

If you are travelling with a breastfed infant, you save the trouble of carrying bottles and bottle sanitization kits. For special food, or medications, you may need to call ahead to make sure you have a refrigerator where you are staying.

34. FEEDING NEEDS OF YOUR TODDLER

With the progression from infancy to toddler, their dietary requirements too evolve. You will have to pack some snacks for travelling time. Fresh fruits and vegetables can be purchased at your destination. Most of the cities you travel to in whichever part of the world, will have baby food products and formulas, available at the local drug-store or the supermarket.

35. PICKING CLOTHES FOR YOUR BABY

Contrary to popular belief, babies can do without many changes of clothes. At the most pack 2 outfits per day. Pack mix and match type clothes for your little one as well. Pick things which are comfortable to wear and quick to dry.

36. SELECTING SHOES FOR YOUR BABY

Like outfits, kids can make do with two pairs of comfortable shoes. If you can get some water resistant shoes it will be best. To expedite drying wet shoes, you can stuff newspaper in them then wrap

them with newspaper and leave them to dry
overnight.

37. KEEP ONE CHANGE OF CLOTHES HANDY

Travelling with kids can be tricky. Keep a change of
clothes for the kids and mum handy in your purse or
tote bag. This takes a bit of space in your hand
luggage but comes extremely handy in case there are
any accidents or spills.

38. LEAVE BEHIND BABY ACCESSORIES

Baby accessories like their bed, bath tub, car seat, crib
etc. should be left at home. Many hotels provide a
crib on request, while car seats can be borrowed from
friends or rented. Babies can be given a bath in the
hotel sink or even in the adult bath tub with a little bit
of water. If you bring a few bath toys, they can be
used in the bath, pool, and out of water. They can also
be sanitized easily in the sink.

39. CARRY A SMALL LOAD OF PLASTIC BAGS

With children around there are chances of a number
of soiled clothes and diapers. These plastic bags help
to sort the dirt from the clean inside your big bag.

These are very light weight and come in handy to other carry stuff as well at times.

PACK WITH A PURPOSE

40. PACKING FOR BUSINESS TRIPS

One neutral-colored suit should suffice. It can be paired with different shirts, ties and accessories for different occasions. One pair of black suit pants could be worn with a matching jacket for the office or with a snazzy top for dinner.

41. PACKING FOR A CRUISE

Most cruises have formal dinners, and that formal dress usually takes up a lot of space. However you might find a tuxedo to rent. For women, a short black dress with multiple accessory options will do the trick.

42. PACKING FOR A LONG TRIP OVER DIFFERENT CLIMATES

The secret packing mantra for travel over multiple climates is layering. Layering traps air around your body creating insulation against the cold. The same light t-shirt that is comfortable in a warmer climate can be the innermost layer in a colder climate.

REDUCE SOME MORE WEIGHT

43. LEAVE PRECIOUS THINGS AT HOME

Things that you would hate to lose or get damaged leave them at home. Precious jewelry, expensive gadgets or dresses, could be anything. You will not require these on your trip. Leave them at home and spare the load on your mind.

44. SEND SOUVENIRS BY MAIL

If you have spent all your money on purchasing souvenirs, carrying them back in the same bag that you brought along would be difficult. Either pack everything in another bag and check it in the airport or get everything shipped to your home. Use an international carrier for a secure transit, but this could be more expensive than the checking fees at the airport.

45. AVOID CARRYING BOOKS

Books equal to weight. There are many reading apps which you can download on your smart phone or tab.

Plus there are gadgets like Kindle and Nook that are thinner and lighter alternatives to your regular book.

CHECK, GET, SET, CHECK AGAIN

46. STRATEGIZE BEFORE PACKING

Create a travel list and prepare all that you think you need to carry along. Keep everything on your bed or floor before packing and then think through once again – do I really need that? Any item that meets this question can be avoided. Remove whatever you don't really need and pack the rest.

47. TEST YOUR LUGGAGE

Once you have fully packed for the trip take a test trip with your luggage. Take your bags and go to town for window shopping for an hour. If you enjoy your hour long trip it is good to go, if not, go home and reduce the load some more. Repeat this test till you hit the right weight.

48. ADD A ROLL OF DUCT TAPE

You might wonder why, when this book has been talking about reducing stuff, we're suddenly asking you to pack something totally unusual. This is because when you have limited supplies, duct tape is immensely helpful for small repairs – a broken bag, leaking zip-lock bag, broken sunglasses, you name it and duct tape can fix it, temporarily.

49. LIST OF ESSENTIAL ITEMS

Even though the emphasis is on packing light, there are things which have to be carried for any trip. Here is our list of essentials:

•Passport/Visa or any other ID

•Any other paper work that might be required on a trip like permits, hotel reservation confirmations etc.

•Medicines – all your prescription medicines and emergency kit, especially if you are travelling with children

•Medical or vaccination records

•Money in foreign currency if travelling to a different country

•Tickets- Email or Message them to your phone

50. MAKE THE MOST OF YOUR TRIP

Wherever you are going, whatever you hope to do we encourage you to embrace it whole-heartedly. Take in the scenery, the culture and above all, enjoy your time away from home.

On a long journey even a straw weighs heavy.

-Spanish Proverb

PACKING AND PLANNING TIPS

A Week before Leaving

- Arrange for someone to take care of pets and water plants.

- Stop mail and newspaper.

- Notify Credit Card companies where you are going.

- Change your thermostat settings.

- Car inspected, oil is changed, and tires have the correct pressure.

- Passports and photo identification is up to date.

- Pay bills.

- Copy important items and download travel Apps.

- Start collecting small bills for tips.

Right Before Leaving

- Clean out refrigerator.

- Empty garbage cans.

- Lock windows.

- Make sure you have the proper identification with you.

- Bring cash for tips.

- Remember travel documents.

- Lock door behind you.

- Remember wallet.

- Unplug items in house and pack chargers.

>TOURIST

READ OTHER
GREATER THAN A TOURIST
BOOKS

Greater Than a Tourist San Miguel de Allende Guanajuato Mexico:
50 Travel Tips from a Local by Tom Peterson

Greater Than a Tourist – Lake George Area New York USA:
 50 Travel Tips from a Local by Janine Hirschklau

Greater Than a Tourist – Monterey California United States:
50 Travel Tips from a Local by Katie Begley

 Greater Than a Tourist – Chanai Crete Greece:
50 Travel Tips from a Local by Dimitra Papagrigoraki

Greater Than a Tourist – The Garden Route Western Cape Province
South Africa: 50 Travel Tips from a Local by Li-Anne McGregor van
Aardt

Greater Than a Tourist – Sevilla Andalusia Spain:
50 Travel Tips from a Local by Gabi Gazon

Greater Than a Tourist – Kota Bharu Kelantan Malaysia:
50 Travel Tips from a Local by Aditi Shukla

Children's Book: Charlie the Cavalier Travels the World by Lisa
Rusczyk

>TOURIST

> TOURIST

Visit Greater Than a Tourist for Free Travel Tips
http://GreaterThanATourist.com

Sign up for the Greater Than a Tourist Newsletter for
discount days, new books, and travel information:
http://eepurl.com/cxspyf

Follow us on Facebook for tips, images, and ideas:
https://www.facebook.com/GreaterThanATourist

Follow us on Pinterest for travel tips and ideas:
http://pinterest.com/GreaterThanATourist

Follow us on Instagram for beautiful travel images:
http://Instagram.com/GreaterThanATourist

>TOURIST

> TOURIST

Please leave your honest review of this book on Amazon and Goodreads. Please send your feedback to GreaterThanaTourist@gmail.com as we continue to improve the series. We appreciate your positive and constructive feedback. Thank you.

METRIC CONVERSIONS

TEMPERATURE

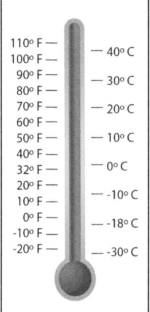

110° F —	
100° F —	— 40° C
90° F —	— 30° C
80° F —	
70° F —	— 20° C
60° F —	
50° F —	— 10° C
40° F —	
32° F —	— 0° C
20° F —	
10° F —	— -10° C
0° F —	— -18° C
-10° F —	
-20° F —	— -30° C

To convert F to C:

Subtract 32, and then multiply by 5/9 or .5555.

To Convert C to F:

Multiply by 1.8 and then add 32.

32F = 0C

LIQUID VOLUME

To Convert:...................Multiply by
U.S. Gallons to Liters................ 3.8
U.S. Liters to Gallons 26
Imperial Gallons to U.S. Gallons 1.2
Imperial Gallons to Liters....... 4.55
Liters to Imperial Gallons 22
1 Liter = .26 U.S. Gallon
1 U.S. Gallon = 3.8 Liters

DISTANCE

To convert ....Multiply by
Inches to Centimeters 2.54
Centimeters to Inches 39
Feet to Meters...................... .3
Meters to Feet 3.28
Yards to Meters 91
Meters to Yards 1.09
Miles to Kilometers 1.61
Kilometers to Miles............ .62
1 Mile = 1.6 km
1 km = .62 Miles

WEIGHT

1 Ounce = .28 Grams
1 Pound = .4555 Kilograms
1 Gram = .04 Ounce
1 Kilogram = 2.2 Pounds

TRAVEL QUESTIONS

- Do you bring presents home to family or friends after a vacation?

- Do you get motion sick?

- Do you have a favorite billboard?

- Do you know what to do if there is a flat tire?

- Do you like a sun roof open?

- Do you like to eat in the car?

- Do you like to wear sun glasses in the car?

- Do you like toppings on your ice cream?

- Do you use public bathrooms?

- Did you bring your cell phone and does it have power?

- Do you have a form of identification with you?

- Have you ever been pulled over by a cop?

- Have you ever given money to a stranger on a road trip?

- Have you ever taken a road trip with animals?

- Have you ever went on a vacation alone?

- Have you ever run out of gas?

- If you could move to any place in the world, where would it be?

- If you could travel anywhere in the world, where would you travel?

- If you could travel in any vehicle, which one would it be?

- If you had three things to wish for from a magic genie, what would they be?

- If you have a driver's license, how many times did it take you to pass the test?

- What are you the most afraid of on vacation?

- What do you want to get away from the most when you are on vacation?

- What foods smells bad to you?

- What item do you bring on ever trip with you away from home?

- What makes you sleepy?

- What song would you love to hear on the radio when you're cruising on the highway?

- What travel job would you want the least?

- What will you miss most while you are away from home?

- What is something you always wanted to try?

- What is the best road side attraction that you ever saw?

- What is the farthest distance you ever biked?

- What is the farthest distance you ever walked?

- What is the weirdest thing you needed to buy while on vacation?

- What is your favorite candy?

- What is your favorite color car?

- What is your favorite family vacation?

- What is your favorite food?

- What is your favorite gas station drink or food?

- What is your favorite license plate design?

- What is your favorite restaurant?

- What is your favorite smell?

- What is your favorite song?

- What is your favorite sound that nature makes?

- What is your favorite thing to bring home from a vacation?

- What is your favorite vacation with friends?

- What is your favorite way to relax?

- Where is the farthest place you ever traveled in a car?

- Where is the farthest place you ever went North, South, East and West?

- Where is your favorite place in the world?

- Who is your favorite singer?

- Who taught you how to drive?

- Who will you miss the most while you are away?

- Who if the first person you will contact when you get to your destination?

- Who brought you on your first vacation?

- Who likes to travel the most in your life?

- Would you rather be hot or cold?

- Would you rather drive above, below, or at the speed limited?

- Would you rather drive on a highway or a back road?

- Would you rather go on a train or a boat?

- Would you rather go to the beach or the woods?

TRAVEL BUCKET LIST

1.

2.

3.

4.

5.

6.

7.

8.

9.

10.

NOTES

Printed in Great Britain
by Amazon

42275606R00071